HELL UNDER

The Lyme Pit Explosion, Haydock, Lancashire.
26th. February 1930.

Ian Winstanley

Landy Publishing
2000

ISBN

1 - 872895 - 54 - 9

British Library in Cataloguing Publication Data.
A catalogue record of this book is available from the British Library.
Layout by Ian Winstanley Tel (01942) 723675

Published by;-
LANDY PUBLISHING
Telephone (01253) 895678

Printed by Nayler the Printer Ltd, Accrington,
Tel:- (01254) 234247

Also from Landy Publishing

The Moorfield Pit Disaster by Harry Tootle
Lancashire Lingo Lines, dialect poems edited by Bob Dobson.
Wrigley's Writings: Poems and Songs by Bernard Wrigley.
Lancashire Bonds, Poems by Alan and Les Bond.
Rishton Remembered by Kathleen Broderick.
Clitheroe Ablaze with Glory by Sue Holden.
Blackburn Tram Rides by Jim Halsall.
Blackburn's Shops at the Turn of the Century
by Matthew Cole.
An Accrington Mixture edited by Bob Dobson.
Lancashire This, That an't'Other by Doris Snape.
Lancashire Laugh Lines by Kay Davenport.

A full list of available titles from
Landy Publishing.
'Acorns', 3, Staining Rise, Staining, Blackpool, FY3 0BU
Tel/Fax:- (01253) 895678

SURFACE PLAN OF LYME PIT

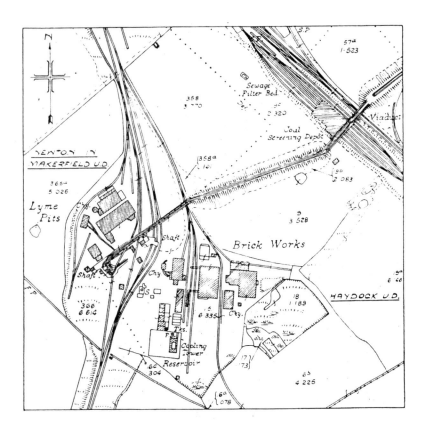

A Glossary of Mining Terms

Afterdamp
Poisonous gas, mainly carbon monoxide, which is formed after an explosion underground.

Bars
Horizontal supports of wood or steel, supported by props to support the roof.

Break
A crack in the coal or rock.

Blocks
Large pieces of wood used to build chocks.

Boxes
Wheeled vehicles run on rails underground. Usually transporting coal. (See Tubs).

Canch
Step left in the roof after the coal has been removed. (See kench).

Chocks
Stack of wooden blocks to support the roof.

Clod
Type of roof rock

Coked dust
Coal dust that becomes hard when exposed to heat.

Conveyor face
Tunnel with a conveyor belt which takes the coal away from the coal face.

Deputy
Mines official with responsibility for working of an area of the mine.

Downcast
Shaft down which fresh air and men are conveyed down the pit.

Filling boxes
Shovelling coal into tubs or boxes.

Firedamp
Inflammable gas , mainly methane, found in coal which becomes explosive when mixed with air.

Fireman
Official in charge of a face or district of a mine.

Goaf or Gob
The space left where coal has been extracted.

HT
High tension electric leads.

Inbye
Towards the coal face.

Kench
See canch

Longwall
A method of working coal from the face commonly used in the 1930's with coal-cutting machines.

Outbye
Away from the coalface.

Pack
A dry stone wall made to support the roof.

Pan conveyor
A machine to transfer coal underground.

Props
Vertical supports to the roof of pine three trunks.

Rippings
Taking down the roof to make height. (See canch and kench).

Shale
Type of soft roof rock.

Tubs
The wheeled, iron vehicles which ran on underground rails to covey material and coal throughout the mine.

Upcast
Shaft which conveys the foul air from the workings to the surface.

Weighting
Pressure of the rock on the roof of tunnels.

CONTENTS

LIST OF ILLUSTRATIONS

AUTHOR'S NOTE.

This is the story of the explosion that took place at the Lyme Pit in Haydock on the 26th. February, 1930. It is written from the official records of the events, the Mines Inspectors' Reports, the Report of the Official Inquiry into the disaster, the local newspapers of the times and last but not least the recollections and memories of the people who were directly involved.

Through my researches, sixty years on, I was able to put together an accurate account of the events in Haydock in February, 1930. In talking to the people who were involved, many of them losing some member of their family in the disaster, it became increasingly obvious to me that this was the time to write the account of the explosion but not the time for it to be published. The scars of the tragedy were all too fresh in people's minds and the book could not be published while those living had such painful memories rekindled. The book was written in 1990 but it for this reason that it has not been published until now.

I would like to express my grateful thanks to everyone who helped in compiling this record, especially the Local Studies Librarians at St. Helens. I would also like to record my thanks to the staff of Wigan Local History Library; to Alan Davis of The Lancashire Mining Museum; the Forshaw family; Protector Lamp and all the people who took the trouble to talk to me in Haydock and share their personal recollections and feelings of the disaster. For many of them it was painful to recall. To them I am very grateful and I felt a great sense of privilege at the time and which time has not diminished.

My purpose in writing about such tragic events is to record accurately what happened in the village of Haydock in February 1930, now that the Lancashire coalfield and its pits are consigned to memories.

Ian Winstanley. December 1999.

1

INTRODUCTION.

It is sixty years since the grim years of the Great Depression when work was scarce and demand for coal so slack that many a pit worked only three days a week. It was against this background that disaster struck Haydock in Lancashire, situated between Wigan and St. Helens. It was typical of many small mining villages in the Lancashire coalfield. Coal had been mined there for many years under the directions of Richard Evans & Co., who owned all the collieries in the village and which were collectively known as '*The Haydock Collieries*'. The Lyme Colliery was one of five belonging to the Evans Company. They were Golborne, Parr Nos. 4 and 5 also known as Southport, Old Boston and Wood pits.

The village was no stranger to the disasters that so often accompanied the mining of coal and there had been explosions in Haydock Collieries in 1868 and 1869 at the Queen Pit and the notorious explosion at Wood Pit in 1878 which, for many years held the grim record as being the worst disaster in the Lancashire coalfield with the loss of 189 lives.

The Lyme Colliery had a chequered history. Sinking had started in 1876 and had reached a depth of 110 yards when there was a serious water problem due to the geological conditions. The pumps of the time could not keep the shaft free from water and the operations were abandoned.

By 1912 the technology of sinking shafts had improved and the work was continued. Many large surface buildings were completed for the processing of the coal that would be mined but the sinking work was again halted by the Great War. Sinking was resumed in 1919 when again there were further developments in the technology of sinking shafts. Concrete was pumped into the shaft walls to control the flow of water from the feeders. This technique proved very successful and the colliery at last began to produce coal in 1922.

There were three shafts in use at the time of the disaster. Nos.1 and 2 were being used for coal winding and the No.3 shaft was used as a pumping shaft. The No.1 downcast shaft that was started in 1876, was later widened from sixteen feet to eighteen feet in diameter and reached the Florida Seam in 1922 at a depth of 395 yards and

2

wound coal from the Higher Florida seam. The No.2 shaft was sunk to the same depth and was the upcast shaft. Coal from the Potato Delf and the Wigan Four Foot seams were wound in it when the Potato Delf seam was intercepted. Both shafts had steam winders which raised two deck cages which held three 12.3 hundredweight capacity tubs per deck. The No.2 shaft was 18 feet in diameter and reached the Florida seams in 1922. At the surface new coal screens were installed in 1923 and a coal washery was completed in 1926.

About a quarter of a mile east from the shafts, a large fault with an upthrow of 240 yards to the east, interrupted the strata and brought the Wigan Four Foot seam, in which the explosion occurred, nearly to the same level as the Potato Delf seam. The Wigan Four Foot seam was recovered by a pair of stone drifts or tunnels driven across the fault from workings in the Potato Delf seam. At the time of the explosion the workings of the Wigan Four Foot seam and the roadways in the Potato Delf seam connected the workings with the shafts. These workings are known as the *No.1 West District* of the No.2 Lyme pit.

Immediately adjacent to the fault and for some distance beyond it, the seam was developed by headings driven in the solid coal. At a later stage a longwall machine-cut conveyor face was opened out from a level known as the '*Conveyor Level.*' This included a short length on the deep side of the level. The face was 100 yards in length and was advancing nearly parallel with the line of full dip of the seam at a gradient of 1 in 5.5. Both the coal cutting machine and the conveyor engine were driven by compressed air which was also used for drilling shot holes, and for auxiliary haulage and pumping in the district.

The Wigan Four Foot Seam had a floor of shale, a roof of coal one foot ten inches thick. The coal was four feet eight inches thick and the floor was of fireclay. The shale roof went on for sixteen yards above the seam where a bore hole had proved the existence of another coal seam. A boring downwards had also proved a third seam of coal at a similar distance below the Wigan Four Foot seam.

The supervision of the colliery was carried out by the following staff:- Mr. Frederick Basil Lawson the General Manager and Agent of all the collieries of Messrs. Evans and Company Limited Mr. Harold

3

Whitehead, the manager and Mr. C.M. Coope, undermanager of the No.1 pit.

At the time of the explosion, the post of undermanager of the No.2 pit had been vacant for five months and an underlooker, John Francis Pickett, who held a Second Class Certificate of Competency, was performing the usual functions of an undermanager in the No 2 pit on a temporary basis, but he had not been formally appointed undermanager. In addition to the undermanager, there were nine firemen in the pit, four on the day shift, two on the afternoon shift and three on the night shift. Normally during the afternoon and night shifts, the workings were not visited by any official superior to a fireman. This was a point that attracted the attention of Mr. Wynne at the Official Inquiry into the causes and circumstances of the explosion. The inspection required by the Coal Mines Act, 1911 was to be made within two hours of commencing work in any shift and usually was made by the fireman of the preceding shift who wrote the report.

Flame safety lamps were general used throughout the workings, but electric lamps were issued to coal cutting-machinemen, conveyor panmen, drillers and fitters. A few working men were provided with two lamps.

Shots were fired in the rippings and in the coal in the No.1 West District. The permitted explosive used was 'Polar Viking Powder' with No.6 H.T. detonators. Shots were fired on all of the three shifts, but in no great numbers except on the night shift, during which an average of about twenty shots were fired by a shotfirer to bring down the freshly cut coal. There was a shotfirer on the day shift to fire shots as required in the Conveyor Face and in the pillar workings to the dip. Firing on the afternoon shift was confined almost entirely to the rippings and it was done by firemen without assistance.

The quantity of coal dust in the face and on the roadways does not appear to have had a very great effect and in accordance with the provisions of the 1920 General Regulations, it was diluted by the application of 'Chance's Mud', a carbonate of lime which was a waste material of certain chemical processes which had been proved to be suitable for the purpose. In a period of six months prior to the date of the explosion, 'Chance's Mud' was distributed in the roadways of the mine at the average rate of 2lbs. per ton output of coal. Inert dust was applied daily by hand in the roadways of No.1 West District and in the face, prior to the firing of shots in the coal. The dust was applied by means of a blast of compressed air from a pipe placed in a bucket of dust at the intake end of the face. Investigations by the Mines Research establishment had found that inert dust suppressed the spreading of coal dust explosions.

General supervision of the stone dusting arrangements was exercised by an assistant of the Agent, who was responsible for taking samples and for having them analysed. When the results of the analysis were known, they were given to the manager and he was then responsible for seeing that remedies were applied in any case in which they were necessary.

The Wigan Four Foot seam in which the explosion took place was a seam which was recognised to give off firedamp freely but in these workings, the general ventilation of the mine was so good that firedamp was rarely present in sufficient quantity to be detected on the flame of a safety lamp. However after the opening of the longwall conveyor face, the first heavy weighting was accompanied by water being driven into the workings and a very large volume of firedamp which, for a short time, overpowered the ventilation current and compelled a temporary suspension of work in the district for several days. The warnings had been given.

The roof in the conveyor face was supported by steel *'props'* (tubes with a timber core) and corrugated *'bars'* or *'straps'*. The roof in the roadways was supported, where supports were required, by steel arch girders which were used right up to the face of the *'caunches'* in the Conveyor Level and the Main Slant. A considerable length of the Main Brow was also supported in this manner. In the pillared portions of the district, where the top coal was left up as a roof, little artificial support was necessary but where support was required, props, or props and bars, were used as well as a *'chock'* here and there.

These were the conditions in the Wigan Four Foot seam prior to the explosion. This was a time when the new techniques of mechanised mining were being introduced to the industry. These new methods had to be learned by the men whose wages depended on how

5

much coal they could produce. It was a working environment in which mistakes could be made and shortcuts taken.

Model illustrating shaft sinking in water-bearing strata by the Francois Process and showing patented reinforced concrete lining.

THE EXPLOSION.

The explosion, which occurred in the main haulage way of the No.2 pit about 6.15 p.m. on Wednesday 26th. February 1930, was the worst in the Haydock Collieries since the Wood Pit explosion of 1878. Forty five men on the afternoon shift went down the pit at 3.10 p.m. and were due to be on the surface again by 11 p.m. The explosion of firedamp occurred in the Wigan Four Foot seam following the firing of a shot. The first that was known of the disaster on the surface was when a telephone call came from a man, Arthur Burrows.

Five men were killed by the full force of the initial explosion which occurred on a conveyor face where compressed air was being used. Twenty six men were injured and fourteen escaped from the workings. The first reports of the explosion in the local press appeared under the headline '*The Lyme Pits Disaster. Growing Death Toll*'. The rising death toll was a sad feature of this disaster as so many of the men were very badly burnt and injured. They were got out of the pit alive and taken to local hospitals where some of them subsequently died.

An early official statement from the Evans Company stated;-

"A local explosion of firedamp following the firing of a shot in the Wigan Four Foot seam at Lyme Pit, Haydock last night took place in the evening. Rescue parties headed by the General Manager, Mr. F. B. Lawson, Mr. D.J. Whitehead, the manager and Mr. C.M. Coope descended the mine and proceeded to the seat of the explosion."

Directors of Richard Evans and Company, Colonel Pilkington and Mr. Gardener were told of the disaster by telephone and went to the pit as soon they could. H.M. Inspectors of Mines, Mr. Davies and Mr. Roberts quickly arrived at the colliery and took an active part in the rescue operations. All the men in the pit had been withdrawn after the explosion and everything that could be done had been done for the unfortunate victims.

On going into the mine, Mr. Lawson, the agent, found that the coal was burning in two or three places and the workings were filled with

7

smoke and fumes. The party had to put on gas masks and carry oxygen bags on their backs. In addition to the fumes, the rescue party had great difficulty in getting to the injured as there were some very nasty falls of roof and more than half a dozen tubs which were standing near the scene of the explosion had been reduced to a twisted mass of broken metal and wood.

In a later press interview, Mr. Lawson said that shots had been fired in the Wigan Four Feet mine in the No.2 Pit and soon afterwards there was an explosion. The men who were nearest were badly burnt and others many yards away were thrown against the walls of the pit and badly scorched as the burning atmosphere flashed round the workings.

A local female doctor, Dr. Winifred Bridges, described as '*a good looking and comparatively young woman of athletic build*' went into a mine for the first time in her life and did heroic rescue work as she tended the injured underground. In the 1930's women doctors were not common and the fact that she went down a mine in these circumstances was a very notable event. She won a place in the hearts of the mining community of Haydock when she went below ground to tend to the injured. She was the daughter of a well known Wigan solicitor and came to Earlestown about three years before during the influenza epidemic and the assistant to Dr. C.J. Mouncey who described her as, '*the most skilful medico in the district at the time.*'

On the night of the explosion she was in the surgery about 6.30 p.m. when the call came for medical help at Lyme pit. She contacted Miss. Bone, the Matron of Haydock Cottage Hospital and both of them went in the doctor's car to the pit about three quarters of a mile away. The journey was made in darkness, by the side the railway lines and along rough paths.

When they arrived at the colliery they saw the colliery officials at the pithead with Dr. Dowling of Haydock and Dr. Jones of Ashton. Dr. Jones had just recovered from a serious illness and it was impossible for him to go down the pit. Dr. Dowling had served the people of Haydock for many years as a general practitioner and as the Medical Officer of Health. He had often been down the pits to injured miners but he was not a young man and Winifred Bridges had no hesitation in going down the pit with him.

Dr. Bridges, reluctantly, gave her account of the events to the *'Newton and Earlestown Guardian'* reporter;-

"They gave us miners' lamps and we went down in the cage to the bottom of the shaft. After that we went along the colliery road. We found ourselves walking, and occasionally climbing, over boxes which had been strewn about the roadway after the explosion. We had to travel like this for about three quarters of a mile, stooping in the low portions. We came to the scene of the explosion where we met colliers carrying a stretcher on which lay a man with a broken leg. By the fitful light of the miners lamp Dr. Dowling and I put the limb in splints and made him as comfortable as possible. Our work went on in the pit for an hour and a half and we put arms and legs and fractured thighs in splints and was to the men's injuries as best we could. We saw the bodies of three men who had died before we got into the pit and when we got to the pithead again we found Miss Bone doing valuable work in assisting the injured men before they were removed in the ambulance. It was an extraordinary experience and one I do not wish to have again but I would do it again if necessary."

Mr. Forshaw was very impressed with Dr. Bridges as were many in Haydock and further afield. He said she went straight down the pit to the face and never hesitated, stayeing down for about an hour and a half until everyone was attended to. The first two bodies which the party found were huddled together under a big iron tub large enough to carry 15 cwt. of coal. The bodies were terribly mutilated and difficult to recognise. A further three dead were found at the face, badly disfigured. The colliery was fairly clear of fumes except for the last 100 yards to the face.

Other first hand accounts of the rescue work were given to the press. Sammy Forshaw, of Common Row, Earlestown, was called from his bed to help in the rescue operations and was accompanied by John Gaskell a worker in a neighbouring pit. He said the pit was about 500 yards deep and 900 yards under the surface. The explosion

9

occurred at the coal face. He went down the pit with fourteen other men including Mr. Kay, Paddy Crehan, Mr. Whitehead, the manager, Mr. Coope, the assistant manager, Mr. Lawson, the general manger, Colonel Pilkington, Dr. Dowling and Dr. Bridges.

One of the men involved, Jack Burrows, was comparatively uninjured. He was knocked out by the explosion and had the presence of mind to crawl through the inky blackness, his lamp being useless. He went through the stone and dust and got to the telephone about twenty yards from the face to give the alarm. This was the first news of the disaster and he was able to tell his story to the press;-

"I owe my life to the fact that I had just left the spot where the explosion occurred, to have a drink of tea. We had just finished one job and we were waiting further orders. No sooner had I left my working place that I heard the terrific explosion. This was followed by a blinding flash and a thick wall of coal dust seemed to come towards me. I was temporarily blinded but I had an electric lamp and immediately returned to see if I could help any of my mates. I came across one of my pals. He had been badly injured and was burnt about the body and his clothing ripped off. I took off my shirt and wrapped it around him and then crawled back to the telephone and inform them at the haulage house of what had happened.
I then started to make my way back to see if I could do anything to help some of the injured men, but before I had gone many yards I collapsed and the next thing I knew was that I was in company with Bert Chick and two other men and I was being attended to at the bottom of the pit shaft."

Following an article commemorating the sixtieth anniversary of the disaster, journalist Alan Whalley of '*The St. Helens Star*' was contacted by Mr. Pat (Paddy) Crehan. Alan invited me to go with him to interview Mr. Crehan who said he had been down the pit at the time of the explosion, though not in the explosion area. I was privileged to hear, first hand, his account of that day. At the time Mr. Crehan was eighty five years of age and looked and talked like a very young fifty year old even though a life in the Haydock mines had taken its toll on him.

This is a transcript of interview recorded 12th. March 1990. Pat Crehan told me;-

"Well, we was up in the other end of the pit near the workings. We were a long way from the blast at the time. It was going down a thousand yards, down a one in four dip. That was the West Side and to here was on another level ran over the top of it here and we was going in this way in what was called Potato Delph. This was at right angles to the explosion area and the distance from that point at which the met there at the top to where we were working was about two miles in. If you looked above us I should say we were somewhere under the Vulcan. Later on I become a deputy and we used to be saving these areas because we were under the Vulcan you see and we had to leave pillars and we had not to touch them. Well that is the area we were in.

We were stopping half a shift. We had gone down the pit and we were down the pit about 6.30 a.m. and we carried on through our work we had to walk as there was no manrider or anything like that, so we had to stop for overtime and we had to stop half a shift then. At about 5 a.m. we were cleaning this place up so that we could get ready for finishing it and the deputy came round. I am not quite sure now what his name was. It was either Martin Hurst or an old fellow named Carney from Golborne. Well, just as he got to us we felt this draft. Like a big rush of air. Well we came to the conclusion then that there had been a fall in the return air road and it had blocked the ventilation, so we said this to the deputy and he could not understand it, so, of course nobody travelled the return air road in them days. It was no tfit for anybody to travel. It was so bad. So we said to him that it would mean somebody going round the air road and he said to me 'I'm not going off that road it's not really fit for me to go round.' Just prior to that, a few months before, one fellow was lost in that air road and he was down there or a couple of days. Well it was a day and a night. He was alive when they found him in the dark. It was Billy Mannion from Old Boston.

But anyway, from then we decided that we were going out and we had finished our shift and we knew that there was something wrong but we did not know what until we got closer where the Potato Delf met the West Side and that was close to the pit bottom. At the pit bottom and there was an old man there named Bill Wilde. He was an afternoon on-setter and he got timber down and one thing and another for the following shift.

But before I go any further. There's a fellow that I want you to make a note of, who, in my opinion and everybody's opinion, at that particular time was the hero of the day. His name was Tommy Hughes. He lived at the latter end and I do not know whether he is now dead or not. He was in that district where the explosion was. He came out and got to the pit bottom and notified them that the explosion had taken place. There was only old Bill Wilde there and he told them to get word up pit and tell then to get the Boothstown men, the Rescue Brigade.

Anyway, Tommy Hughes went back when he had given the warning into the workings. He was going to see what he could do. He went down there and anyway we came out and we did not know that this had happened with Tommy. We went down and there was four of us together and there was Joe Higgins, of Park Road, Bill Hardman, he was from Park Road as well and there was a Wally Duckworth. He came from Grosvenor Road. He was supposed to be one of the rescue men you know. I think he was supposed to be a trained man for this rescue work. I lived in Lime Street at the time.

So we went down and when we get to the bottom of the incline we went into the level where the face was. Going into that, we came to a place where everything was ablaze and we did not know what to do or anything. You see we were strangers in a strange part of the pit and we'd all come out with no tools or anything and the result was, what we should have had really was bags of stone dust to put this fire out but we had nothing but Wally Duckworth had a road hammer and he was trying to pluck it all out where it was all ablaze the timber. You know when they put the arches in they cover it in with the timbers so that it will not fall down on the road you know. So he was trying to rip it out with the road hammer. Well it was no good. He was trying to do the impossible. Well, we said, 'We'll never put this out,' so we decided to go in, further in, and when we got further in it had faded out the fire part. Died off. It had been agate that long, I mean burning when we were going in. In every arch in the centre of it there they are joined together at the centre with two plates and bolts in them you know. Well it had heated these bolts up that they started pinging, coming past us as if there was somebody firing a bloody gun at you.

Anyway we got in and we came to this fellow who was dead there as we came through. We looked at him and we didn't know who the hell it was. He had got that much of the explosion you know. All his face was all grey and his eyes burnt out. Well with one thing and another we got a stretcher and put him on a stretcher. There was no stretcher there we had to go and root for one and we put him on the stretcher and there was just four of us then and we have to come up then thousand yards plus this other road. Up there one in four. Up, carrying a chap on the stretcher. It was a pretty tough job for us.

As I say by the time we got to the pit bottom with this fellow in this stretcher. It must have been about 10 o'clock when we got to the pit bottom with this fellow on the stretcher. We had been down there since about six in the morning, so by the time we got there we got him in the cage and old Bill Wilde was there and we got up the pit. As soon as we got up the pit they were taking him out of the cage you know. Two of us had to stand back so there was two of us at either handle. So I stood back, Lawson was there, Thompson, everybody all these big bugs and everybody, Doctor Dowling and Doctor Bridges. I didn't know that the doctors were there at that particular time because my idea was to get home and get out of it and so was the others.

Unfortunately for me, Lawson came to me and he said, 'Have you just come from the explosion area?'

I said, 'Yes.'

'Right,' he said, 'Just get in this cage again and escort the doctors down to the explosion area.' Well I had to get into the cage again. Lawson went down with us. He was the agent, the manager of all the Haydock Collieries. He was the big boss. I had to down again and we went down with Bridges and Dowling. When we started off I stopped at the top of this incline and gave lights to doctor Dowling and Dr. Bridges and I said, 'Now I'll lead the way. You follow on.

What I want you to do, is to get your lamps.' There was no electric lamps then you know. They were oil lamps and I told them to get their lamps and I'd dress 'em up so that they would not blink one another. Well we went down this incline you know, so I put them a blinker upon it. Binkers on the back of the lamps. I'll just show you what I mean with that."

At this point Paddy got up to get his old miner's lamp and showed me how the flame could be shaded by moving a section of metal round the glass so that the person holding it would not have the flame shining directly into their eyes.

"So I says, 'In certain places as we are going down it will be a bit low, so when I say keep down, you'll know what I mean. It will be low.' Well we did not do so bad until we get to a certain point where it gets a bit low and I said, 'Keep down here Doctor'. I gets down and he is following me and he must have got up a little bit too soon and he hit his head on a girder and ends up on his arse. I'm not sure now if it didn't knock his lamp out but any way it didn't stop us from going on irrespective of whether it knocked his lamp out or not. Doctor Bridges didn't hit it, she realised what it was when Doctor Dowling did it. So anyway we carried on until we got to where I should say half a mile off the explosion area and I said to Doctor Dowling, 'Now you will be able to fix up here for your station so pick your places.' Anyway they found a spot a bit wider than normal and I didn't know whether they had anyone with them carrying splints and medical supplies because they had enough to do in getting down there. I should imagine that there was somebody at back of them but I could not see.
It was hot there and sulphur and everything. Well I never eat anything when I came up for about three days my stomach was that bad you know with the fumes and everything. But a soon as I delivered the doctors into where they were I said, 'Well I'll get back home now' and off I went.
Well I met a fellow named Hughes coming down. He was a deputy then in the pit and he had been in Earlestown enjoying himself somewhere and having a night out and I met him and he was coming running down, dressed up as

though he was going to a ball . He had come straight down the pit grabbed a lamp and was running down to the explosion area. Wilf Hughes was his name. He lived in Grange Valley.

When I eventually got to the top of the pit my father was there waiting. He had been running round to the hospital because he had got word that I had been fetched out and taken to the hospital and he had run to the hospital. Well he saw the nurses and the matron there and told him I was not amongst the casualties. Anyway he came running back to the pit then. Nobody knows. This was at 12 o'clock midnight. I was eighteen hours down the pit and you know I had to go and see manager about getting my bloody overtime in. They had not booked my overtime. They were in them circumstances as no one was checking out.

If I am not mistaken I think that there were two or three pit ponies down there and the pit ponies were all right. Nothing happened to the pit ponies. They was on a different level, higher up you see. I was thirteen when I went down the pit. I stayed down until I was 63, fifty years. I finished up at Boston with the Training Centre. The last pit was at Wood Pit. I was deputy at Lyme Pit for a while and then I came to Wood Pit."

The evacuation of the dead and injured from the mine was speedy and efficient. An official statement was issued at 11 p.m. on Wednesday by Mr. Lawrenson, the general manager of Richard Evans & Co, who had come from down the pit after being involved in the rescue work. The statement said;-

"At 6.15 tonight an explosion of firedamp owing to shot-firing occurred in the Wigan Four Foot Seam. A party headed by the General Manager (myself) and the Manager, Mr. Whitehead, and the undermanager, Mr. Coope, made a descent of the mine and organised a rescue party. Two small fires were put out and the injured were brought to the surface on stretchers. The mine had been cleared by 11 p.m. The casualties are 5 killed and 20 in hospital with burns and shock, the others were able to proceed home."

There were ambulances waiting at the surface when the men were brought out. Matron Bone, who had gone to the colliery with Doctor Bridges, was there and administered first aid before the injured were taken to hospital. There were so many casualties that the St.Helens Hospital had to be asked for help and some of the injured were transferred there.

The sad scene at the pithead was captured by a reporter of '*The Newton and Earlestown Guardian*' who was obviously very moved by what he was seeing. The crowd had had a long wait for news of their friends and loved ones.

"Heart-rending were the scenes near the pit shaft when over a thousand relatives and friends were keeping acts of vigil. It was a horrific sight to see the tear stained faces full of hope and yet fear as the solemn stretcher-bearers filed past. There was no moon and only the glow of the colliery lights. The hiss of steam and the clouds of smoke brought the pallor of death to the scene. Mothers, whose sons were not yet out of boyhood, had gone to the pit on that afternoon shift, to hear news of their dear ones and were told, 'No news yet.' Everywhere there was the impression of eagerness but we could only wait and see. The waiting continued. They did not know. They could not say. It was wiser to spare the pain..
At the shaft itself there was a crowd of officials all waiting helpless until the rescue party came up. 'Make way,' they cried. With a rumbling the door opened and a solemn, grimy faced Lancashire lad backed out and then another. A gentle heave and the stretcher with its dreadful burden came into view. Not a sound. Not a word. Only bowed heads here and there and a hat or two removed. Some poor mother's son passing for the last time from the colliery to be interred this time in a grave not so deep or as large as the one from which he had just emerged and one that would smell sweetly of flowers.
At the slow pace, the five stretchers bearing five corpses which, but a few short hours before, had been full of joy and living. The crowd looked on and wondered how men could give their lives for the lives of others, for their sacrifice was as great as any warrior that laid down his life for another."

A survivor told the press of his experiences as he was having his injuries dressed at the surface;-

"We were ready to take coal from the coal face when I heard a rumbling at the far end of the pit. There was a terrific pressure of gas and someone shouted, 'Firedamp'. I heard one or two men cry out and with a couple of others, I rushed down but could not get near the scene of the explosion. We were driven back by the fumes and we struggled to the pit face. Someone telephoned from above and when I donned a fire mask. I helped to drag out some of my friends. It was terrible to have to drag them out like that when a few moments before I had been talking to them."

Accounts of what had happened below ground were given to the press by the injured men who were released from hospital after treatment. James Sowerbutts was sent home suffering from shock and he told reporters;-

"I went through the War but never through the whole of that time did I have such a terrible experience. We were like rats in a cage and we went home shaking. I vowed, during the experience, that if I got out alive, and there were periods that I had my doubts, I would never go down again but now I realise that that was foolish talk. It is our only living and we had to take the chance of earning a living with both hands these days and I am sure that it was a pure accident and there was no negligence about it.
I was working in a dip in the road and had just left my mate to draw a tub. When I got about ten yards away there was a terrible crash and everything seemed to be falling about my ears. I was unable to speak and after a minute or so I heard my mate calling, 'Are you all right, Jim?' but I could not answer. Again he called and I was able to shout back to him. We them both made towards the commotion where we thought there might be a way out, but after running about one hundred and fifty yards we were overcome by the gas and fumes and forced to turn back. We ran on the opposite direction and met the rescue party. We reached the scene of the accident and there we picked up some of the injured man and decided to get together, Everyone was wonderfully

patient and all willing to do their best for the injured, Somewhere we heard voices calling, 'Don't leave me. Don't leave me,' and once again we tried our best to find a way out. We half carried and half dragged the injured with us but several times we were forced to lie down to get fresh air. I was nearly dropping when we did eventually reach the brow. Keenan, whom I had been carrying, was my first care as I knew I was not seriously injured. One of my mate's hands was terribly cut and burnt and he eventually fainted. Some of those reported injured must have been in the rescue party. I know almost all the men in the district but I don't recognise some of the names."

Two brothers named Hennigan spent four hours searching the mine for their brother Jack, who had descended the mine during the afternoon. They did not see him among the injured and he had not returned home after the accident occurred. They made their frantic journeys to the hospitals and back again to the mine and finally their search came to an end when it was discovered that he was among the dead who had, up to then, not been identified.

Some of the men who were taken to the Haydock Cottage Hospital and were treated for their injuries were later allowed to go home. They were, James Sowerbutts of Newton Road, Parr, Albert Lowe of Juddfield Street, Haydock, Arthur Burrows of Cherry Street, Earlestown and William Plant of Clipsley Lane, Haydock.

Arthur Burrows, aged 23 years, of 26, Cherry Street, Earlestown was in the explosion area when it occurred. He scrambled and crawled two hundred yards over debris to the telephone and raised the alarm on the surface. He was exhausted when rescued and was taken home suffering from severe shock and the effects of gas. His statement to the press read;-

"I have worked down the mine for about two years. Just after six o'clock I was having a drink when I heard a loud bang and a big black cloud rushed towards me and I was thrown six or seven yards backwards but I managed to get up and scrambled and crawled along the ground for perhaps 200 yards. On the way I had to climb over overturned tubs and when I came up some of the fellows were nearly done up

and I carried on to the telephone as the urged me on. It seemed like hours to me but it was about twenty minutes to cover the two hundred yards. George Parr and Bill Muldowney found me and took me to safety."

Another collier who had a lucky escape was William Plant, of 272, Clipsley Lane, Haydock. He was filling boxes at the time of the explosion and he could not say what time it was but he thought it about seven o'clock. He was working in a place that was about eight feet high and about the same in width. He said,

"I could see nothing. Like a fog of dust came across me and I went as best as I could to the shaft. I was working with James Cunliffe of Clipsley Lane who was killed and Ogden of Ashton-in-Makerfield. Near us were Garbutt of Parr and Albert Lowe of Juddfield Street, Haydock. The shock mesmerised us for a moment or so and drove us back. We put our caps over our noses and mouths and used them as gas masks. After several attempts we made our way from the Cinder Brow to the main haulage way. We met a party of injured men and one of them was Duggie Conway who was badly injured and almost worn out. We were not much better ourselves but we did what we could. The men were badly burnt and had little clothing left. They were shouting for help. We only missed being burnt to a cinder."

Clambering over the 15 cwt. tubs which had been swept over by the force of the explosion almost blocking the way, they were met by a second rescue party led by a fireman named Spurgeon Green of Grosvenor Avenue, Haydock. The lamps were going out and they were going along in single file. Plant continued;-

"I had a man in front of me and one behind and we would not leave go of each other. The one behind me, I don't know who he was, said 'Don't leave me' and I said 'I'll not so long as I can keep on."

James Cunliffe, who lived opposite the Cottage Hospital, was another who got out of the explosion area. He was suffering from shock and the effects of gas. He was working with William Plant when a cloud of gas bore down on them. It was so bad that they used their caps to cover their noses and tried to make their way out. They met a party of thirteen men all of whom were badly burnt and together they stumbled over tubs and staggered along rather dazed.

"We had done all that we could for the injured men. I have never seen anything so terrible as the sights I have seen in that pit. It was the most terrible sight I have ever seen and I never want to see it again."

Continuing out of the pit, he said he came across the youngest casualty in the disaster, Kenneth Forshaw, only 17 years of age, who was suffering badly from his injuries but he kept a stiff upper lip and they gave him drinks and rallied him. James Cunliffe stated that at that time he never thought that they would get out of the pit alive because the smoke and gas were so bad.

Dr. Dowling paid tribute to all who were involved in the rescue operations;-

"I cannot speak too highly of the way the management and the men handled the situation. Dr. Bridges was eager to go down and help the injured men as soon as she heard of the accident. When we arrived there was no need to wear gas masks, but when we reached the bottom of the 500 yards deep pit, we little knew what to expect when we reached the spot where the explosion had occurred. As we made our way along the pit roads, we were met by miners carrying a dead man. This did not deter our party and a few moments later a seriously injured man was carried past, our only thought was to render immediate assistance. We made our way to the place where the explosion had occurred and we found three dead men. They had all been burnt and asphyxiated. Our immediate thought was for the living men who were found lying in the workings. It was a tremendous task to deal with the men and we worked like Trojans to alleviate their sufferings and get them to safety. For more than three hours we were down the pit. Dr. Bridges stood up to the strain wonderfully well and refused to leave the pit until we had done all that was humanly possible."

Eight of the injured died in the local hospitals as a direct result of their injuries. The medical treatment that they received was primitive compared to that we have today. The final death toll reached thirteen.

Interior of power house, Lyme Pits.

THE VICTIMS.

All the men in the immediate vicinity of the explosion were badly burnt and had coal dust fused with their skin in addition to broken limbs which had been caused as they had been thrown around by the violence of the explosion. One man was so badly charred that he was identified until late on Thursday morning.

Clement Elliot, of 28, Burley Street, Newton-le-Willows, was in the Haydock Cottage Hospital, swathed in bandages, only recognised by the fact that he was known to have a nail missing on his big toe.

The five killed in the initial explosion were;-

James Cunliffe, aged 34 years, married, fireman, 164, Parr Stocks Road, St.Helens.
Roundel Cecil Page, aged 20 years, single, daywageman, 36, Vista Road, Haydock,
John Hennigan, aged 38 years, single, haulage hand, 37, Cherry Street, Earlestown,
Frank Thomasson, aged 37 years, single, daywageman, Rumford Street, St.Helens,
William Seddon, aged 33 years, married, collier, 7, Vista Road, Haydock.

The injured were taken to Haydock Cottage Hospital and St.Helens Hospital with terrible burns. Eight who were taken from the pit alive later died of their injuries. They were;-

Kenneth Forshaw, aged 17 years, single, a haulage hand of 342, Park Street, Haydock, and the youngest of the victims. He had extensive burns. Died 28th February.
William Conway, aged 45 years, married, a collier of 86, Athol Street, Earlestown, who had extensive burns. Died 28th February.
John Foy, aged 39 years, married, a daywageman of 35, Birch Street, Newton Common, who had extensive burns and a fractured thumb. Died 28th February.
Albert Page, aged 29 years, married, daywageman, of 30, Vista Road, Earlestown, who had extensive burns. Brother of Roundall. Died 1st March.

22

Clement Elliot, aged 49 years, married, a daywageman of 28, Burley Street, Newton-le-Willows, who had extensive burns. Died 2nd. March.

George Hollis, aged 43 years, married, a putter-on, 17, Regents Avenue, Haydock, who had extensive burns. Died 7th. March.

George Franklin, aged 43 years, married, 13, Grange Valley, Haydock, a collier who had extensive burns. Died 9th. March.

William Molyneaux, aged 45 years, married, 48, Clarence Street, Newton Common, a collier who had extensive burns. Died 19th March.

Albert Page died in St. Helens Hospital, the rest in Haydock Cottage Hospital. Those who were injured were;-

George Herbert Chick, aged 34 years, a pumper who suffered burns and a fractured leg.

Francis Keenan, aged 22 years, 7, Bay Street Golborne, a collier who was burnt.

Sidney Marsh, aged 44 years a New Boston Cottages, Haydock, a daywageman who was burnt and had severe head injuries.

Arthur Pilling, aged 25 years, 354, Clipsley Lane, Haydock, a fitter suffering from burns.

John Duffy, aged 40 years, 11, Clipsley Lane, Haydock, a daywageman suffering from burns.

James Clarke, aged 26 years, a coal-cutter man suffering from burns and a fractured thigh.

Thomas McGuire, aged 39 years, Mercer Street, Newton-le-Willows, a contractor also burnt.

Joseph Muldooney, aged 42 years, Birch Street, Newton Common, a panman suffering from burns.

John Brown, aged 25 years, a coal-cutter man who had burns and a fractured leg.

Thomas Clarke, aged 34 years, 30, Fleet Lane, Parr, a coal-cutter men who had burns and fractured thigh.

These men were treated in Haydock Cottage Hosptal and those below at St. Helens Hospital.

John Bell, of 28, Newton Park Road, St.Helens.
George Herbert, of Church Road, Haydock.
James Parr, 41, Providence Street, St. Helens.

With the human toll of the disaster known it was for the formal inquest to ascertain the cause of death of the thirteen men. There were two inquests, one at which the formal evidence of identification was taken and one to determine the cause of their deaths and there was also an Official Inquiry into the circumstances and causes of the disaster commanded by the Secretary of State for the Mines Department.

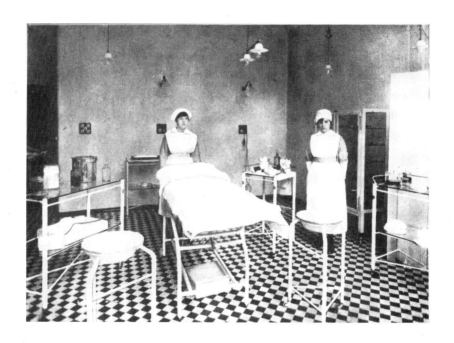

The operating theatre, Haydock Cottage Hospital

24

.154

Richd Evans & Co., Limited.

Haydock, Ashton, Edge Green, Parr, & Golborne Collieries.

TRUCK ACTS. 1831 to 1896.

Name................ *Ken Forshaw*

Date................1930

		£	s.	d.
Days	...........at......	1	4	3
Yards	...........at......			
	...........at......			
	...........at......			
	...........at......			
Overtime				
Subsistence Wage Award ...	...		4	3
GROSS WAGES £		1	9	3

Deductions and Payments made at request of Employees :	s.	d.
1 Rents		
2 Fire Coals		
3 Explosives		
4 Lamps, Oil and Trimming		
5 Tools		
5A Drilling Machinery		
6 Tallies		
7 Permanent Relief Society		
8 Haydock Cottage Hospital	2	3
9 N. Health & Pensions Insur.		
10 Unemployment Insurance		
11 Benevolent Fund		
12 Recreation Ground		
13 Best Fire Coal		
Total Deductions and Payments ...		
Paid in Cash £	1 6 6	

The above Wages are 1911 Rates plus 32 %.

Kenneth Forshaw's last pay check

25

Some of the survivors

Photographed in the grounds of Haydock Cottage Hospital.

Back Row
Herbert Chick, Frances Keenan, Sydney Marsh, Arthur Pilling

Front Row
John Duffy, James Clark, Thomas Maguire, Joseph Muldooney.

THE FIRST INQUEST.

The inquest was opened by Mr. F.A. Jones, the Deputy County Coroner, in the billiard room at the Waggon and Horses Hotel, when evidence of identification was taken and the proceedings adjourned until the 14th. March. Mr. Samuel Brighouse, the County Coroner, should have conducted the proceedings but he was indisposed. Mr. Brighouse knew Haydock well. Over a period of many years, it had been his sad duty to conduct inquests in the village on men and women who had been killed or died because of accidents in the mines. There was a strong bond of mutual respect between the villagers and the old County Coroner.

After expressing his personal sympathy to the relatives of the dead Mr. F.A. Jones read a message from Mr. Brighouse, in which he expressed his sympathy at the disaster and was sorry that he could not conduct the inquiry as he was suffering from a cold. He went on to say;-

"Would you say to the relatives of the poor dead fellows that I am sorry. They will know what I mean. I say this. During the many years that I have held inquests it has been my unfortunate task to be present at many colliery disasters and I never do so without wishing that some means could be designed to prevent them. The Lancashire collier is a brave fellow, a man of character, and one who is always prepared to carry out his duty to the best of his ability. He will always do anyone a good turn. I have a great admiration for the Lancashire collier and I can safely say, we like each other. Tell them at the inquest that I am full of grief for those that are left behind and we all appreciate the great usefulness of those who labour in coal mines and that they shall be assured that an impartial inquiry into the circumstances of the explosion and the manner of their deaths and we pray for their souls departed."

At this first session of the inquiry, evidence of identification was taken from the relatives of the dead. John Victor Page, a driver, of 36, Vista Road, Earlestown, said that Roundel Cecil Page was his brother. He had worked in the pit for only two weeks and he had made no complaints. Mary Cunliffe said that James Cunliffe, a

27

fireman of 168, Parr Stocks Road, was her husband aged 34 years. He was in good health when he left for the pit.

James Hennigan, father of John, of Cherry Street was asked by the Coroner if he could identify his son who was 38 years of age. John replied, *"As well as I could."* The Coroner commented, *"Yes, I know he was a horrible sight."* The identification was done with the aid of James' teeth and his clothes.

Edward McClory said Frank Thomasson lodged with him at 34, Rumford Street, St.Helens and he had identified him. William Seddon was identified by his young wife Winnie of Vista Road.

P.C. Albert Doran told the court he first received notification of the explosion at 8 p.m. on Wednesday 26th. February at Haydock Police Station and went to the pit. He found all the injured men were badly burnt.

Mr. Lawson, the general manager of the Haydock Collieries, expressed sympathy on behalf of Richard Evans and Company. The secretary of the Miners' Association said that were many brave deeds done below ground that day and he would like to express sympathy to the grieving relatives.

With the formal identification over, the court was adjourned to a future date when the causes of the men's deaths would be examined. Meanwhile the grieving relatives could bury their loved ones. The funerals of the initial victims took place against news of those who died from their injuries. An air of sadness and gloom prevailed in the village.

John Hennigan was interred at St. Mary and St. John Roman Catholic Church, Newton and there was a large and tearful crowd at the service. There were more sad scenes in Earlestown on Wednesday when Roundel Page and Albert Page of Vista Road, were buried at the Earlestown Cemetery. Hundreds of people with umbrellas lined Crow Lane and stood under grey skies to show their respect.

The funeral of William Conway drew a large crowd. He left a widow and eight children and his coffin was covered with the British

Legion flag. The service was at the Parish Church in Newton-le-Willows and conducted by Reverend Lees.

On the 4th March, in Haydock, the mourners were standing outside as the youngest victim, Kenneth Forshaw aged 17 years, of Park Street, Haydock was laid to rest. His coffin had rested in the vestry of St. Marks' Church during the weekend and fifty of his old work mates attended the funeral. The 1st. Haydock Company of the Boy's Brigade, to which Kenneth belonged, was present and as the procession passed along Clipsley Lane all the huse window blinds were lowered. Children lined the route. After a short service at which the Reverend Wilkins officiated. Kenneth was buried in the same grave as his mother who had died some years before.

William Seddon's funeral took place in Earlestown. There was a large crowd in Vista Road and the funeral procession passed through streets lined with people showing their respects to Ashton Methodist Church at Stubshaw Cross. After the service, the coffin was taken to Heath Road churchyard for burial. William left a widow and one child.

RELIEF FUND EFFORTS.

At a meeting of Newton-in-Makerfield Urban District Council, T.B. Ball, the Chairman, said that the Haydock Council had asked them to contribute to the Relief Fund for the dependants. This motion was passed. Haydock Urban District Council formed a committee and asked people to contribute as generously as possible. Contributions from the respective districts would be received by Messrs. Dickenson and Ashcroft at the Council offices in Haydock.

An early list of contributions appeared in the local papers;-

Mr. and Mrs. McCorquadale	£30 - 0s - 0d.
Mr. W.H.Dixon.	£5 - 0s - 0d.
Cllr. Denby	£2 - 2s - 0d.
Cllr. Lloyd.	£2 - 2s - 0d.
Cllr. Baines.	£2 - 0s - 0d.
Cllr. Norcross.	£2 - 2s - 0d.
Lord Mayor of Leeds	£2 - 2s - 0d.
C. Brown.	£2 - 2s - 0d.
Cllr. Taylor.	£2 - 2s - 0d.
C. Dickenson	£1 - 1s - 0d.
T. Ashcroft.	£1 - 1s - 0d.
J. Evans.	£1 - 1s - 0d.
H. Norcross.	£1 - 1s - 0d.
J. Cooke.	£1 - 0s - 0d.
J. Forshaw.	£1 - 1s - 0d.
R. Taylor.	10s - 0d.
A nob	5s. - 0d.
Total	£56- 14s 0d.

Local publicans Mr. R.P. Griffin and Mr. J. Keen made collections in their houses for the Relief Fund. They also sent floral tributes to the funerals with the balance of coppers put into the Hospital Box.

The Wood Pit explosion of 1878 left many Haydock widows and orphans destitute, without a breadwinner. They were totally reliant on payments from the 'Haydock Explosion Fund' The late 1890's saw the passing of 'The Workmen's Compensation Act' by which the victims of mining accidents could apply for compensation through the Courts. In the 1930's the Unions were much stronger and looked after their members in these circumstances.

THE RESUMED INQUEST.

The inquest was opened at the Colliery School in Haydock with a large attendance of local people and mining experts. The Deputy Coroner, Mr. Jones presided over the proceedings. Also present were Mr. Charlton, the Divisional Inspector of Mines, Mr. Coatsworth, Mr. Davies and Mr. McBride, the Inspectors of Mines. The inquiry opened at 10 a.m. with a break taken for lunch. On returning, the business went through till 4 p.m. when the verdict was returned.

Addressing the jury, the Coroner said that the inquest was being held to find the immediate cause of the deaths of the victims and to find out how those deaths came about. He instructed the jury;-

"If you find the deaths were caused by explosion, then you can say how the explosion was brought about. If you satisfy yourselves how brought about then you will have to satisfy yourselves if it could be avoided. You have only two verdicts, 'Misadventure' or 'Manslaughter against the individual'. In this court, however you can say anything that will save life in the future. If you return a verdict of misadventure I will ask you if you have any recommendations to make which will be carried out."

Mr. Peace, solicitor, on behalf of the directors of Evans and Company repeated his message of sympathy and referred to Miss Bone of the Haydock Cottage Hospital as a *'ministering angel'*. Evidence was given as to the cause of deaths.

With the formalities over, the court got down to the business of looking for the reason for the men's deaths.

Several men were able to add to the story of what happened underground immediately after the explosion. The first was Clarence Edbrook, the manager of Lyme pit No.1, who lived at 212, Haydock Street, Earlestown, who said he was called from his home at 6.20 p.m. on the 28th. February. When he descended the mine, he noticed two coal fires and two dead bodies. Thomas Hughes then joined him and they found the body of Cunliffe, the fireman, about thirty yards from the face. They then came across a man with a broken leg and he told the witness that there were two further up. They went to search and

31

found Thompson but there was little hope for him. His electric light was still burning.

Spurgeon Green, said he was a fireman at the colliery who had worked in the mine for twenty three years and had been a fireman for twelve years. He was at work on the day of the explosion in the No.2 district and left at 5.45 p.m. having been delayed by repairs that had to be done. He was going towards the pit bottom, when he suddenly felt a change in the ventilation. He was about one hundred yards from the seat of the explosion and by his watch it was 6.02 p.m. He knew that an explosion had occurred in the No.1 District and he gave orders that phone calls should be made to the hospitals. He said Mayor was the first man out of the No.1 and then he came across John Folley twenty yards down. He had three others with him suffering from shock, one of them was Thomas Hughes.

John Canny, contractor, of Vicarage Road, Haydock had worked in the pits for thirty years and stated that he had found no gas when he made an inspection. After the disaster Cunliffe, the deceased fireman, had come towards him and the dust nearly choked them. He turned off the compressed air and went to look for Hennigan. Elliot and Conway then stumbled up to him and Elliot's feet were on fire.

Thomas Hughes a haulage man who resided at 5, Fleet Street, Golborne went to Hennigan and later heard a report and all the lamps were blown out. He got a lighted lamp off another man and Jack Parr who were running down.

James Colly of 68, Bank Street, said that a little gas was found a long time ago and when he began work at Lyme pit. He understood that the Rules of Colliery stated one shot had to be rammed and fired at a time.

The course of the inquiry then turned to the question of shotfiring in the mine and Mr. Lawson, the agent was called. He said he was surprised to find four other shot holes charged at the scene of the explosion. In reply to a question from the Divisional Inspector of Mines he said that after the explosion, he examined the place and found that a shot had not been fired but four shot holes where charged. This did not necessarily breach the Coal Mines Act but it was against the rules of the colliery. The orders given by him were, that only one shot had to be charged and fired at one time. Mr. Lawson added that the shots were vertical and not horizontal as they should have been. Apparently it was easier to drill vertically than horizontally.

Mr. Harold Whitehead, the manager of the colliery, also gave evidence of the events underground during the rescue operations. He came across Albert Page and had to ask who it was. Page said he was *'not so grand'*. The manager continued along and found four shot holes with the detonators hanging out and he knew that it was against orders. The witness described, with diagrams, the pattern of the shot holes and showed how a break ran right across the coal over the holes.

Mr. Cook, the Miners Secretary and Mr. Jack Jones, Secretary of the Yorkshire Miners Federation took up the questioning of Mr. Whitehead and pointed out that there were regulations stating, *'that no shot should be fired unless it be inspected by a fireman with an approved safety lamp and satisfied that there was no gas within a radius of twenty yards.'* If there was a cavity where gas could be lurking then the shot should not be fired. Mr. Whitehead said that he had seen a break in the coal. The seam had been opened about two years ago and there had not been much gas since it had been opened. The manager stated that Cunliffe, the fireman, had booked the number of detonators before the accident at twenty and fifteen were found in his tin.

Mr. Whitehead continued;-

> *"I was not there when the shots were fired and I do not know if the regulations were carried out but the holes were all together and against my orders. I came here from Abram Colliery and have been mining since about 1900."*

It was put to him that he was responsible for seeing that the regulations were carried out. There were vertical holes drilled by the contractor who was paid by piece work.

John Francis Piggott of 306, Newton Road had worked in the mine for twenty eight years. He had earlier tested for gas and found it all right and he accepted the fireman's report. On Thursday he noted a little gas and noted four shotholes that had been drilled. He thought the shot had been fired at night and did not think that the four vertical holes contributed to the cause of the accident.

The Verdict

The formal verdict read as follows;-

"Death due to misadventure, through ignition of gas unforeseen by the fireman."

To this the jury saw fit to add the following five riders.

1). We think the work in the district in the afternoon is too much for one fireman.
2). We are of the opinion that the stemming of more than one hole at a time is a common practice and should be stopped.
3). We are of the opinion hat under no circumstances should coal be thrown into the gob.
4). We strongly object to vertical holes being drilled, as we think it is not always possible to stem the holes satisfactorily.
5). We are also of the opinion the His Majesty's Inspectors should visit the mines more frequently.

The verdict of the Coroner's jury was formally recorded but the cause or causes of the disaster was to be examined by the formal Government Inquiry.

BEST

HAYDOCK
5565
St HELENS

AND

HOUSE

GAS

STEAM

COAL

For HOME, EXPORT and BUNKERS

34

THE OFFICIAL INQUIRY.

The official inquiry into the disaster was ordered by E. Shinwell, Esq., M.P., Secretary of State for Mines. The report was made by Mr. F.H. Wynne, B.Sc., H.M. Deputy Chief Inspector of Mines and submitted to Mr. Shinwell at The Mines Department, Dean Stanley Street, Millbank, London, S.W.1, on the 12th. September, 1930. The full report was subsequently submitted to Parliament.

The inquiry was opened in the Council Chamber of the Town Hall, St, Helens on Tuesday 29th. April and went on until Friday 2nd. May, 1930. There were many eminent people from the mining fraternity at the proceedings, including Mr. Charlton, H.M. Divisional Inspector of Mines, Mr. McBride, H.M. Senior Inspector of Mines), Mr. Edwin Peace of Messrs. Peace and Darlington, Solicitors of Liverpool, representing Messrs. Evans and Company, Mr. Lawson, the agent and Mr. Whitehead, the manager of the Lyme Colliery. Mr. Henshaw, J.P., F.G.S., M.Inst.C.E. represented the Institution of Mining Engineers. Professor Wheeler, appearing for the Safety in Mines Research Board, Mr. Arthur Roberts and Mr. James Hilton attended for the Lancashire and Cheshire Colliery Undermanagers and Underlookers Association; Mr. Cook and Mr. Joseph Jones represented the Miners' Federation of Great Britain and Mr. John McGuirk, and Mr. Foster for the Lancashire and Cheshire Miners' Federation. Mr. Frowen represented the Federation of Colliery Firemen's and Deputies Association of Great Britain; Mr. Miller and Mr. Hesketh for the Lancashire and Cheshire Colliery Deputies Association.

The witnesses who gave evidence at the inquiry were Percy Harold Fairclough, surveyor; Thomas Caunce; William Hughes; Spurgeon Luther Montague Green and James Carney, all firemen, John Francis Pickett, colliery underlooker; Claud Bernard Platt, Superintending Testing Officer at the Mines Department Testing Station; James Clarke, coal cutting machineman; Ernest Pilling, fitter; Francis Keenan, collier; Arthur Burrows, panman; Thomas Hughes, haulage hand; Horace Edwards, lampman; Thomas David Davies, Junior Inspector of Mines; David Coatesworth, Junior Inspector of Mines; Thomas Lindsey McBride, Senior Inspector of Mines; Richard Vernon Wheeler, Director of the Safety in Mines Research Board

Experimental Station; Frederick Basil Lawson, colliery agent and Harold Whitehead, manager of Lyme Pit.

A detailed account of the events leading up to, at the time of, and after the disaster was heard by the inquiry and it was confirmed that five men were killed outright and twenty three others were injured by the explosion. Of the injured, eight later died from shock due to sever burning. A plan showing where the men were found after the disaster and their positions at the moment of the blast was submitted to the court.

Wind and Fire
The explosion caused a temporary reversal of the air current accompanied by a cloud of dust in the intake air road and up the downcast shaft. It also caused a temporary reversal of the air current in the main road to other parts of the pit.

The evidence collected after the explosion showed the passage of the force and flame in the roadways. This showed that there was a lot of flame in the Conveyor Face and some force but the flame produced by the explosion was the more destructive. It came outbye along the Conveyor Level for only a few yards. It must have found its way out by the Main Slant in which, prior to the explosion there were seven brattice screens. These were completely destroyed. At the main junction of the Main Slant to the Pump Dip there were indications that it stopped although there were indications of force further inbye which was evidenced by damage to a set of trams. Flame apparently extended outbye along the Main Brow as far as the fault for near this point the timber lagging of the steel arches supporting the roof and sides of the haulage road was found to be on fire in three places.

In other places, there were indications of great force after the explosion. A train of full tubs in the slant at the entrance to the Conveyor Level had been pushed in the brow near the junction and had been flung about. At the junctions of the Main Slant and the Main Brow with the Conveyor Level, the chocks had been dislodged and the single blocks scattered all over the place. In the Main Brow the air crossing, built of steel joists and concrete, had been lifted bodily from its setting and collapsed in fragments on the floor. No doubt the force was augmented here by the obstruction caused by the bends in the path of the blast and also by the tubs standing in the roadway.

Under God's Protection

A strange feature commented on by the inquiry and mentioned by Paddy Crehan years later, was that two ponies stabled in the Conveyor Level in stalls which consisted of only a few props and battens covered with brattice cloth nailed to them and only 120 yards from the coal face, were not injured at all and the flimsy erection in which they were housed showed no signs whatever of any disturbance.

The majority of the men near the conveyor face, after they had recovered from the initial shock of the explosion and the air current had resumed its original course, were able to find their way out towards the Main Brow where they were met by the injured and later by parties coming into the pit.

A Cool Head

A fireman, Spurgeon Green, who had worked in the No.2 District and who took the initiative in organising exploratory operations and the relief of the injured, was complimented by the inquiry. He sent men to the surface and gave instructions for the messages to be sent by telephone to the agent and the manager asking for ambulances and medical assistance as well as helpers.

The Cause

After hearing of the general conditions in the pit after the explosion, the inquiry then turned its attention to the question of the cause of the disaster. There was no doubt or difference of opinion at any time either as to the point at which the explosion originated or to its cause. It was caused by the firing of a shot of Polar Viking Powder in the caunch of the Main Slant which was in fact the main return airway from the conveyor face. This was proved by the evidence given to the inquiry by James Clarke, a coal cutting machine attendant, who was present with the deputy James Cunliffe when the shot was fired. Clarke said in evidence that he was sitting besides Cunliffe when the shot was fired. He saw him turn the handle of the firing box and the explosion followed. He was with two other coalcutter men, Clarke and Brown. Clarke's evidence proved conclusive and it was corroborated by what was found after the explosion. The position of the shot cable and the battery, the rammer and the handle of the battery and the body of the dead fireman and the signs of force and coking, all proved that this is what had happened.

It was a rare event that men who had seen an extensive pit explosion survived to tell the tale. The evidence of Clarke and Ernest Pilling, a fitter was so graphic and interesting. James Clarke was questioned by Mr. Charlton who asked him, *"Did the fireman Cunliffe come to you shortly before the explosion took place?"* Clarke answered, *"Yes."*
"That is the first time he came to you, was it, to tell you that he was going to fire some shots?"
"Yes."
"What did he tell you to do? Did he tell you to go down the face?"
"Yes. We went with him."
"He took you down the face?"
"Yes. He took us down the face."
"Did he lay down the cable at the same time, or had he done that before?"
"Laid it at the same time."
"I see. He laid it at the same time?"
"Yes."
"Did you see the fireman make any test for gas?"
"No."
"Where was your machine?"
"A good deal away from me."
"Was your machine at the top side of the slant of the face below?"
"Well, just below."
"Below?"
"Just below the slant."
"And did you se the fireman make any tests for gas?"
"Well, I did not notice that."
"You did not take notice of whether the fireman made any test for gas?"
"No."
"All you know is that he took you down the face with him?"
"Yes."
"All the three of you?"
"Yes., all the three of us"
"And he laid the cable out at the same time?"
"Yes."

"Did you see him attach the cable to the battery or did you take no notice?"
"No."
"Where did you stay when he fired the shots?"
"We sat besides him."
"Will you tell us what happened?"
"He fired the shots. We saw him turn the handle."
"And what followed then?"
"An explosion by fire."
"What happened after that?"
"Well, I know nothing after that. He said 'Go for your lives chaps; something has happened."
"Did you see anything?"
"Yes. I saw fire. I saw fire coming out."
"From where?"
"From the kench. I saw fire coming out.".
"On the face and it was coming down towards you?"
"No. It went in a little on the slant. I saw it lit up."
"You saw a glimmer first and then the flame?"
"Yes."
"And at what stage did he say, 'Go for your lives chaps' or whatever he said?"
"He said, 'Go for your lives something had happened."
"Was that as soon as you saw the glimmer?"
"Yes."
"What did you do? Did you leg it as fast as you could?"
"I legged it. I did for sure. If you had been on the face at the same moment, you would have legged it too."
"You legged it down the face and what is the next thing you recollect happening?"
"I remember nothing after that."
"Do you remember going away from the danger?"
"Yes, I remember nothing after the fireman caught me."
"What was the next thing you remember, waking up in hospital?"
"No, I wakened up on the face after that."
"That was the next thing you remember after that? You had been unconscious had you?"
"No, I was not unconscious; I was only out for a bit."
"What happened to you?"
"I was blown towards the face."
"You fell forward did you?"

"Yes."
"What was the condition of the atmosphere? Did you feel any scorching or pain?"
"I felt burns."
"A great heat passing over you?"
"Yes, a great heat passing over."
"Did you feel dust in the air at all?"
"No, no dust in the air."
"You did not notice any particular dust?"
"No."
"But you saw this glimmer first and then the hot flame seemed to come down towards you and you feel the pain of the burning. Now, when that happened did you hear anything as well? Was there any sound?"
"Yes, there was a sound coming out of the slant."
"I do not quite understand it."
"There was a sound going put in the slant before we ran."
"You say there was a sound going out in the slant before you ran?"
"Yes."
"Let me be quite sure about it. You saw the shotsman turn the handle and you saw the glimmer?"
"Yes."
"And you heard something?"
"Yes."
"What was it you heard?"
"We heard the din of it going out."
"What was the sound, or can you describe it at all?"
"Like a gun going off."
"Then after that the flames seemed to come from the face?"
"Yes."

Mr. Wynne, the commissioner asked, *"Was it the sound of a shot or another sound?"*
Clarke answered, *"It was like unpteen shots going together."*
Mr. Charlton continued, *"It was like thunder?"*
"Yes, like rolling thunder."
"When this happened you would be between the pan conveyor and the face?"
"Yes."
"How long did this appear to last then? Did you feel the force of the air blowing down the face at all?"
"No, I felt no air blowing down the face."

"Well, you felt something?"
"I felt the fire coming. That is all."
"But you said that you felt something which made you fall forward to your face."
"Yes. There was the fire. It was the fire."

Clarke was the first witness who had survived the explosion to be examined. The next was Ernest Pilling who was questioned by Mr. Charlton who asked, *" Well now, you were busy working on this job. Was there anything that happened out of the ordinary up to the explosion?"*
"No."
"What happened when the explosion took place? What were your experiences?"
"The first thing I knew was a rolling sound like thunder. Then there was a distinct pause, I should say about 10 to 15 seconds. I heard a report and I jumped up and looked down the face and I saw the flame coming down. I also saw Clarke running before me. I do not remember anything after that."
"At the time you heard a noise like rolling thunder?"
"Yes, a rolling noise."
"How long would it last, would you say, Mr. Pilling. An appreciable period?"
"A second or two, I suppose."
"Not very long?"
"No."
"Then you saw the flame?"
"Yes."
"And you saw Clarke?"
"Yes."
"You say it overtook him and it was on you?"
"Yes."
"As you were working at your job, on which side of the conveyor pan were you?"
"The coal face side."
Mr. Joseph Jones continued the questioning of Ernest Pilling, *"Now you have just replied to Mr. Charlton that you thought there was a lapse of 10 to 15 seconds."*
"Yes."
Have you a fairly clear recollection of what took place then?"
"Well, no. I would not like to give any stated time."

41

"You think that it was a fair assumption, 10 to 15 seconds?"
"Yes."
"Can you take your mind back and try to visualise exactly what happened? Can you recall whether the flame was nearest the pan or the goaf? Can you give us some idea of the actual position coming down?"
"There seemed to be a bluish flash overhead and there seemed to be a red flame following that."
"Would it be nearer the goaf as I have just asked?"
"No, it came the full width of the road."
"Over the pan way and the packs, the full width?"
"Yes."
"Was it deep and spread out close to the roof or low?"
"It seemed to be general thing. The roof seemed to fall."
"Clarke would be about what height? He was in, we have our own ideas about it. You say it caught him up?"
"Yes."
"Round about the head?"
"Yes."
"So that you would say about a foot from the roof?"
"No."
"It seemed to be a general thing. The road seemed to be full of fire coming down."
"Yes."
"The blue flash was overhead?"
"Yes."
"From about the height of Clarke's head upwards?"
"Yes."
"You say the whole of roadway was full of flame?"
"Yes."
"You are quite sure of this?"
"Yes."

Summary

The evidence which these two eyewitnesses gave to the inquiry established to experts that there was small initial explosion immediately the shot was fired, followed after an interval of a few seconds by a bigger explosion. The first explosion caused a large volume of firedamp to be sucked into the slant from crevices in strata and from the cavities in the goaf and it was this firedamp that was ignited by flame from the firedamp left burning after first explosion.

An examination of the caunch after the explosion revealed that the shot hole, bored horizontally, had penetrated a break which crossed the roadway diagonally and extended over the dip side of the pack towards the waste or goaf below. In the shale roof outbye of the caunch, several more breaks existed which were easily seen. There was a further break crossing the roadway at right angles in the top coal inbye of caunch. It was possible that these breaks were interconnected with each other and also with further breaks and cavities in the roof over the goaf on the dip side and over the pack on rise side of the slant. There could be no doubt that firedamp was present in these breaks and cavities.

After the explosion, samples of gas were drawn from some of these breaks at depths varying from twelve inches to four feet six inches by means of a copper tube with a aspirator attached. The firedamp content in some instances was small and almost negligible but in others it was present in proportions that were within the explosive limits of a mixture of firedamp and air. The report commented;-

> *'It was because firedamp is so likely to be lurking in breaks that the charging of a shot hole in which a break has been detected is strictly prohibited.'*

The Commissioner thought that coal dust had played little or no part in explosion. He based his conclusion of the fact that only small samples of coked dust were found. The results of an investigation carried out on a large number of dust samples were collected systematically in the face and roadways after the explosion by Professor Wheeler at 'The Safety in Mines Research Laboratory' in Sheffield. There was also an absence of carbon monoxide in the afterdamp and as far as was known, none of those killed or injured showed any symptoms usually associated with the inhalation of this gas.

There was little doubt that the explosion would have extended throughout all the workings if it had not been for the presence of inert dust in sufficient quantities in roadways. The stone dust was instrumental in confining the effects of the explosion to a comparatively small area.

43

The Fatal Shot

It was very clear that the explosion originated from the firing of a shot which was in contravention of the provisions of Clause 6(d) of Explosives in Coal Mines Order of September, 1913 and amended in 1915, 1919, 1922, 1924 and 1926 which stated that;-

> *"Every shot shall be charged and stemmed by or under the supervision of a shotfirer. Before a hole is charged a shotfirer shall examine it for breaks running along or across and if any such break is found the hole shall not be charged except in stone drifts if special permission has been given in writing by the manager or undermanager."*

It was not clear from evidence whether James Cunliffe, the fireman who fired the shot, made an examination for breaks in the shothole, but he knew that there was a break present. Cunliffe was killed and had no chance to defend himself but his competence as a fireman and shotfirer was not questioned and those who were in a position to speak gave him an excellent character.

Albert Page was the contractor who bored, or supervised boring, of shotholes in the caunch and who bored the shot hole in question. Page was killed and could not give evidence on this crucial point. There was no reason to think that he would not have confirmed the very circumstantial account of the conversation as given by the two witnesses.

Mr. Charlton questioned Spurgeon Green of the events immediately after the explosion when Green and Whitehead arrived at the scene of blast. Spurgeon Green was well known in Haydock. He worked all his life in the Haydock Collieries and was noted for his bandy gait which was due to the fact that he twice broke both legs in accidents at his work. Mr. Charlton asked Green, *"We will go back to where you had gone to face with Mr. Whitehead and you saw him test for gas?"*
"Yes."
"What happened then?"
"Mr. Whitehead, after he had examined for gas, looked underneath the caunch and I assume he saw the wires hanging down."
"You had seen them before?"

44

"Yes. Mr. Whitehead said to me, 'Now then, this is not fair Spurge,' and then all at once a voice replied, 'It was a straight in shot he fired, Mr. Whitehead.'"

"How do you connect that remark from this unknown voice with what Mr. Whitehead said? Mr. Whitehead said, 'This is not fair, Spurge' and the voice answered, 'It was a straight in shot he fired Mr. Whitehead?'"

"When we heard the voice, we looked round to see where it came from and we found out that it came from a man of the name of Albert Page, so Mr. Whitehead said to him, 'Now then Page, what are you doing down here?' and he said, 'I couldn't get out.' Parr had gone for some more assistance to get him out, so Page said, 'I drilled through a break Mr. Whitehead.' Mr. Whitehead asked him if he had informed the fireman. he replied, 'Yes.' The Mr. Whitehead asked him if it had been stone dusted and the man replied, 'No.'"

"Mr. Whitehead, having arrived there, had seen something which made him say to you, 'That is not fair, Spurge.'"

"Yes."

"Did you know what Mr. Whitehead meant by that?"

"I had an idea."

"What was your idea by what he meant by that?"

"That Mr. Whitehead had informed both shotfirers and fireman that they must not ram more than one shot at a time."

"And what was there to be seen? How many shots were there already there?"

"We found four."

"Four wires hanging down?"

"Yes."

"Did you come to the conclusion that a shot had been fired?"

"Well, we had already been told that a shot had been fired."

"Who told you that?"

"Page."

"He said, 'I drilled into a break?'"

"Yes."

"So that you knew that five shots had been charged before one shot had been fired?"

"Evidently they must have been."

"You say, you knowing and everybody knowing, Mr. Whitehead had told you and everyone concerned that shots should never be charged before one is fired, he said to you, 'This is not fair, Spurge,' and you thought what he meant was that he had been let down?"

"Yes, that they disregarded the rule."

"So that he proceeded further to ask about the thing that was in his mind. Knowing a shot had been fired there, he was full of anxiety to know whether everything had been done that might have been done and he asked the men, 'did they stonedust?'"

"Yes."

"And he said , 'No.'"

"Yes."

"I am still rather puzzled as to why Page should have said when he heard Mr. Whitehead's remark, which presumably he did. 'It was a straight shot, Mr Whitehead.'"

"Yes."

"What did you perceive that he meant by that?"

"After we heard the voice and looked round and examined and found what it was, then we came to the conclusion that it must have been a horizontal shot he must have fired according to Albert Page's evidence, according to what he said."

"What you think of this, that Albert Page had some reason why he wanted to assure Mr Whitehead that it was straight in shot."

"Oh, yes."

The Manager's Evidence

Mr. McGuirk questioned Harold Whitehead, the manager of Lyme Pit. He asked Mr. Whitehead, *"Now, you say you saw Page before he was taken out of the pit?"*

"Yes."

"Can you tell us what conversation you had with him?"

"I met Albert Page about 70 yards from the face. This is the first time I saw Albert Page."

"That is on the slant?"

"Yes. Spurgeon Green and Parr were busy with artificial respiration with a man and I saw a man sitting down besides them. I said, 'Who is that?' Either he said, or one on the other side said, 'It is Page,' and I said, 'How are you?' or something like that. I can not exactly remember now. He said, 'I am not so grand but I can walk out.' You are asking me now to repeat all I said at the inquest?"

"Yes, I am asking that."

"Yes, that is right. That is all I said to Page."

"Did you speak to him afterwards?"

"Yes, I did."

"Will you tell us what you then said to him?"

"Certainly. The next time I came in contact with Page was when he spoke to me in reply to a remark I made to Spurgeon on the face of the slant. He heard me say to Spurgeon Green, 'This is not fair Spurgeon,' I did not know Spurge was there at the time and Page replied, 'The hole that was bored, (I am not quite sure whether he said the hole that was fired) was a straight one.' I said, 'Oh,' and he said, 'Yes, I bored into a break with it.' I said, 'Did you tell the fireman?' He said, 'Yes.' I said 'Was it stonedusted?' He said, 'No.'" That is all the remark I had with Page."

Malpractice?

It was evident that shotfiring practice was the root of the problem and it was only natural that a good deal of evidence was led to ascertain whether the shot firing practice at the colliery was in accordance with the statutory requirements. Three firemen were closely examined in this respect but they stoutly maintained that as far as they knew, no irregularities occurred.

Mr. Wynne, the Commissioner, commented;-
"I should have been glad for Cunliffe's sake if I could have come to some conclusion in regard to him and to have been able to suggest that this was an isolated instance of neglect of the statutory requirements on his part. I regret, however, that in view of the evidence, I am unable to do so."

What was established beyond doubt was that the manager and the agent had gone to considerable lengths to warn the firemen and shotfirers about their duties generally and specfically, in particular, on two points connected with shot firing. In the first place, against charging more than one shot at a time and secondly against firing shots in holes bored vertically in the roof. Even with these warnings, in the coal roof under the canch, there were four vertical holes positioned roughly at the corners of a four foot square and every one of these holes were found charged, ready for firing. In addition, two other vertical holes were found uncharged, one in the roof a few feet nearbye.

There was an attempt made by the representatives of the Firemen's Association to gloss over the charging of five holes at once by suggestion that Clause (g) (ii) of the Explosives in Mines Order, inferred that it could be left to the shotfirer to decide whether or not

47

the firing of one shot would be liable to relieve any part of the work to be done by another and that Cunliffe had exercised the discretion allowed to him. This might have been in Cunliffe's favour were it not for the definite instructions that had been given to all the firemen and shotfirers by the management on this point.

Cunliffe's competence as a shotfirer and fireman was not questioned and those who were in a position to speak on the subject gave him excellent references. It was not to be believed that he charged and fired the holes without regard for the possible consequences. In fairness to him, the Commissioner thought it reasonable to suggest that his sense of danger was dulled by the freedom of the air in the vicinity of the caunch from firedamp.

There was little doubt that there were greater risks of firing shots in caunches in longwall workings than in any other situations since breaks were more likely to be formed in the roof strata under these conditions. For this reason therefore, the number of shots fired in such places was the better. It was known that ripping in certain classes of rock could not be undertaken economically without the use of explosives but there were many rippings in which explosives were extensively used and it was thought that it was a moot question whether any advantage was derived from this practice.

From the conditions in the Wigan Four Foot seam, it was suggested that the firing of the shots in such strata could be reduced, almost to vanishing point. It was pointed out that, for some time prior to the explosion, shotfiring had been discontinued at the caunch in the Conveyor Level and it was a matter of regret that it was not discontinued in the Main Slant at the time. Shotfiring the caunches was not carried on after the explosion.

An effort was made by the representatives of the Firemen's Association to establish a case that the district allotted to the fireman of the afternoon shift was too large for him to carry out his statutory duties satisfactorily owing to the pressure to get through the work. It was suggested he was hurried and it was possible that he performed his duties in a hurry.

The fact that steel arch girders were extensively used for supporting the roof in the roadways minimised the effects of the explosion. If props and bars had been used, falls would have occurred and created difficulties of escape and rescue which might have added seriously to the total of dead and injured.

In the 1930's coal faces were becoming mechanised and the new methods called for new arrangements of supervision. Earlier in the report, it was mentioned that during the afternoon and night shifts, supervision was normally exercised by the only fireman who was on duty. No official superior to fireman visited the workings during these shifts.

Mr. Wynne felt that if visits to the workings by superior officials during the afternoon shifts had been the custom in the mine, better discipline would have been maintained and the probability of detecting firemen who were disobeying the very definite orders would have been greater.

Mr. Wynne concluded his report saying;-
"It is not out of place here to mention the firemen and workmen witnesses who gave their evidence at the Inquiry. Speaking from a fairly wide experience, I can say that generally the manner in which they approached the questions put to them and gave their answers was most impressive. They exhibited a degree of intelligence considerably above the average and seemed not only to know exactly what they wanted to say but also how to say it."

With the publication of *'The Report into the Causes and Circumstances of the Explosion which occurred at the Lyme Pit'*, the village of Haydock left the public gaze and was left with its feeling of great sadness and sense of loss.

POSTSCRIPT.

It was reported in *'The Newton and Earlestown Guardian'*, 18th. July, 1930;-

DR. WINIFRED BRIDGES MARRIED.

"Dr. Bridges was married on Wednesday to Mr. Sydney Shaw. They met at the University at Manchester on the congregation filled the Roman Catholic Church of St. Oswald, Ashton-in-Makerfield. The miners had reason to remember her and many miners wives and daughters and pit brow lasses with shawls around their heads greeted the bride when she arrived with her father.
She was smiling and looked very charming wearing a gown of gold façon and peacock train overhung with pink deal chiffon. On her shoulder she wore orange blossom and a dainty halo of pearls. Her bridal veil was embroidered Brussels née and she carried a sheaf of lilies.
The bride is he daughter of Mr. Henry Bridges of Ashton and the bridegroom is the son of the late Mr. Shaw of Oldham. The reception was held and the bride and groom left for their honeymoon in the South of England in a small green baize ensemble trimmed with ermine and a hat to match. The bride, who was at Liverpool University and at Manchester will continue to practise in Ashton"

Years after, there are many in Haydock with fond memories of the young woman doctor who helped their menfolk when their position was so desperate.

A Coincidence

While researching this book at Newton Library, I was looking at old copies of *'The Newton and Earlestown Guardian'* that carried the first report of the Lyme Pit Disaster. A small item tucked away on an inside page caught my eye. It was headed *'The Haydock Explosion Fund'* and went on to say that the balance of the Fund that was established after the Wood Pit disaster in June 1878, fifty two years previously, had been wound up since all the beneficiaries were the dead. The balance of the Fund was donated to the Federation of Lancashire and Cheshire Miners.

FIN

Lyme Pit went on producing coal until its final closure in 1964 when many of the workforce were transferred to the newly opened Parkside Colliery. The inverted concrete funnel of the washery, completed in 1926 was long remembered by the villagers as it stood as a local landmark for many years after the colliery had closed. The site today is derelict and depressing. It is hard to believe that it was at the centre of the country's attention in February, 1930.

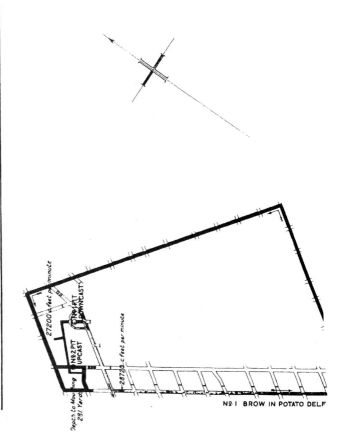

No. I PLAN.

LYME COLLIERY.

PLAN OF WORKINGS IN WIGAN FOUR FEET MINE.

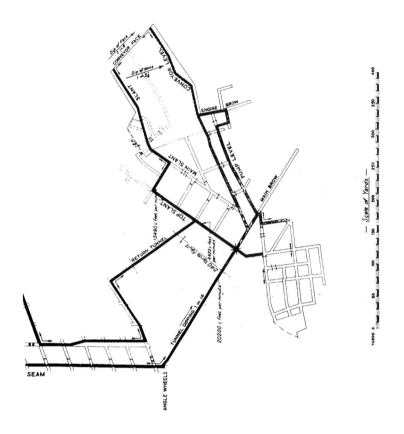

LYME COLLIERY.

PLAN SHOWING SCENE OF EXPLOSION
IN THE WIGAN FOUR FEET MINE

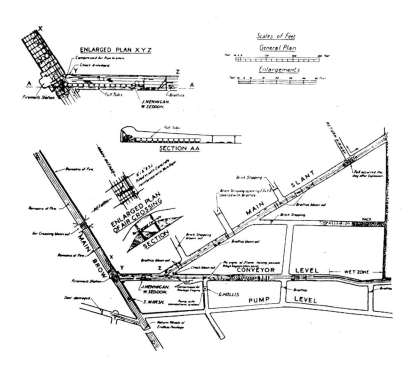

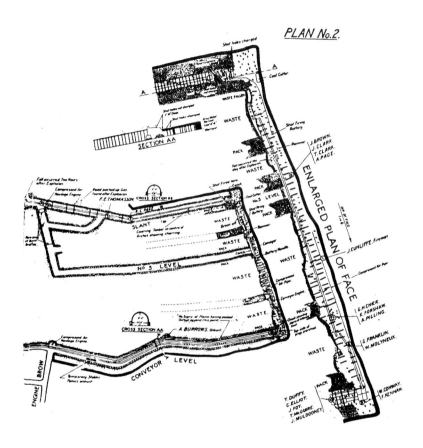